The Child Inside a Liberal

by

Anthony Sebastiano

Introduction

Have you ever noticed how emotional adults of the liberal persuasion become when discussing politics or public policy with those who hold different views? Instead of articulating reasoned arguments, citing facts or examples, liberals tend to become overly excited, sometimes to the point of displaying sadness or hostility. Many contend that such behavior is due to some sort of mental disorder. I offer an alternative view as to why liberals act in this manner. It is my contention that liberals display this type of behavior because they are actually children trapped inside adult bodies. In other words, liberals are adults who possess a child-like mindset. You have likely witnessed for yourself that when alternate views are presented during a debate, liberals will often literally start behaving like children. They will institute the same type of useless defense a child employs when he does not get his way or is caught in a lie, by responding to the opponent's alternate views as mean, cruel, or unfair. Not to mention, being very emotionally sensitive, they tend to yell or scream, in a similar manner to a child having a temper-tantrum; sometimes they even engage in name-calling attacks directed toward their opponents. Often when liberals are losing an argument or are at loss for words, they resort to subterfuge by trying to change the subject. It should be noted that a good number of liberal arguments are peppered with anecdotes, sometimes related somewhat to the topic at hand, but many times not, in a futile attempt to play on the opponent's sympathies and invoke an emotional response. This is because all liberals' solutions to any and all social problems are centered solely on emotions, in the place of rational thought and analysis. You see, liberal adults may be physically mature, but psychologically, they are stuck in a pre-pubescent age. Children who do not learn how to effectively manage their emotions grow up to become liberal adults. Like children, liberals do their best to live a life shunning responsible and deferring accountability for as long as possible. As a consequence, they make every effort to convince the rest of us to also live a life of dependency on someone else. Just like a youngster, who depends completely on his parents for shelter and generally resists the parents' demand to take on increased personal responsibilities, liberals count on others for their economic support. Liberals live in a childhood fantasy world and want everyone else to be as helpless and dependent as themselves. Instead of inspiring people to greater levels of achievement, liberals discourage everyone from reaching their full human potential. Because liberals are immature and uncreative, at least in the sense of establishing sound public policy, it is easier for them to bring everyone else down to the same level as an alternative to encouraging and promoting success. Every liberal has a little boy or girl inside them who has neither accepted accountability nor the harsh realities of life. I will expose the inner child within each and every liberal through various hot political and social issues, as well as the infantile tactics they employ in their fruitless attempt to win an argument.

The Child Inside a Liberal

Chapter 1: Liberal view of life

Liberals have a unique and unrealistic outlook of life in general, very similar to the way a small child views the world. Because the liberal frame of mind is in lock step with that of a young child, liberals errantly believe that they are capable of perfecting and managing the lives of everyone else, resulting in a utopian world where there is no sorrow, no pain, and no struggle. For instance, we all understand that children generally do not possess a proper comprehension or awareness of the dangers of the world. That is why parents tend to caution their young with advice like, *do not talk to strangers*, *look both ways when you cross the street*, or *count the change you receive back from the store cashier*. Similarly, liberals do not see, acknowledge, nor accept the reality that there are others out there who desire to do harm to their fellow man. Likewise, they also ignore the fact that dishonest people exist. You see, liberals refuse to recognize the fact that evil is present in the world. This is probably the reason why young liberals of the Sixties formed communes, danced naked around bon fires, used mind-altering drugs for recreation, and participated in indiscriminate and sometimes bizarre sex acts. They were doing their best to hide from some of the more dreadful aspects of life. Today's liberals may no longer live the commune lifestyle, but they still avoid reality as much as possible.

Have you ever met a happy liberal? There is no such thing, because life itself is something that liberals absolutely loathe. Liberals, in their warped point of view, are so miserable that they constantly try to convince everyone else that human existence on this planet is horrible. Whether the topic is the environment, world population, or race relations, the outlook is always bleak. We have all heard the phrase, *misery loves company*. Because liberals are incapable of being content and find no joy in life, they try desperately to make everyone else just as miserable through warnings of calamity or by attempting to stir up emotions of shame or guilt in others. According to liberals, the sky is *always* falling; the Earth is a rotten, vile place. Therefore, liberals feel the need to constantly berate the public through tales of disaster for partaking in certain activities that they do not approve. For example, when liberals scold those who consume meat products, they warn of an impending doom to the eco-systems that will occur if everyone does not immediately adopt a vegan lifestyle. If fear does not work, they strive to make you feel shame or embarrassment for eating animal flesh by describing meat processing with fables and images of cruelty and barbarism.

Because liberals are naturally unhappy, their beliefs tend to support and even promote activities that produce nothing, is life damaging or even life killing. For instance, liberals tend to unabashedly support abortion, sexual deviation, illicit drug use, and "body modifications", such as extreme, multiple piercings and tattoos. Isn't it interesting how liberals will incessantly shout from the rooftops that the blue whales, baby seals, or spotted-owls need to be saved or protected while claiming it is perfectly okay to abort a human fetus for *any* reason? In the perverted liberal mind, animals are more important than people. Not to mention, liberals try desperately to normalize the abnormal, such as promoting gay marriage or marital units of three of more individuals. They do this by attempting to re-define marriage, frantically trying to convince everyone within earshot that such arrangements are equivocal to the true definition of marriage - one man, one woman - that was established thousands of years ago and is common to all.

It should be no surprise that liberals believe they are smarter than anyone else. It is a defense mechanism to help cover up their ignorance and their misery. Most children at some point in their development go through a phase when they think they are the smartest in the room. Those children who are unable to transition out of this phase grow into adulthood as full-fledged liberals. According to your typical liberal, if everyone would just follow his advice (but not his example) the world would become a place of instant and permanent bliss. If you disagree with a liberal's advice, you will be barraged with ridicule by him and other liberals.

In order to perpetuate the myth that *they* know best, liberals tend to aggregate themselves with other liberals, generally in large cities. I like to call these enclaves, *Liberalland*. Liberals do not seem to mind living on top of one another, which is most likely the reason why they berate those who own houses and possess land. Being surrounded by liked-minded people only fuels their elitist attitudes. As a tactical matter, liberals also surround themselves with those holding similar views so they can attack their enemies en masse, like a pack of wolves. When one liberal's views are challenged, other liberals immediately join in to defend, as well as begin a character assault against the initial challenger. Regardless of whether other liberals support the cause of the initial liberal being challenged, they come together in order to defend and promote liberal ideology. Never let it be said that liberals are real independent thinkers.

Chapter 2:   Liberal view of the U.S. Constitution

Most liberals will not admit this in front of the cameraman. They have *vile contempt* for the U.S. Constitution! This is because the Constitution was purposely designed to impose restraints on federal action and we all know that liberals worship at the altar of the federal government. When a microphone is close by politicians, of the liberal mindset, love to espouse the virtues of democracy that are enshrined in the Constitution. Of course, our Constitution structured this nation as a republic, but that argument is for another day. However, in secret liberals wish they could completely scrap the original Constitution and draft a new one based upon unrealistic liberal values. Why you may ask? Liberals detest freedom, period! Because of their elitist approach, liberals consider us non-liberals stupid and incapable of making *correct* life decisions. Therefore, a new constitution would allow liberals to restrain individual liberty.

Because they hate freedom and the fact that the Constitution was written so that people could govern themselves, liberals do everything they can to paint our founding document as outdated.

One of the ways liberals do this is to relay the false premise that the Constitution is a *living document*. Just like a child who reinterprets rules for his own advantage, liberals profess that the Constitution needs to be continually reevaluated in light of the changing values of each successive generation. Hence, liberals persistently try to twist the meaning of constitutional wording in order to find some bogus justification, through judicial ruling, to either overrule laws they do not like or create new "laws" that they cannot pass through appropriate legislation.

In reality, the Constitution does not ever need to be reevaluated or reinterpreted, because it was written to guard against the frailties of human nature, which are unchangeable. By design, mechanisms were put in place within the Constitution to ensure those given the power of government do not abuse the privilege of their public service. The Founding Fathers did provide an amendment process as the means for altering the Constitution under extraordinary circumstances. This process was intentional fabricated to be slow and laborious in order to protect freedom. Since liberals, wanting immediate gratification, are just as impatient as children, they are unwilling to follow proper procedures for amending the Constitution. Instead, liberals prefer to circumvent the process through judicial activism.

Liberal view of the First Amendment

Liberals like the First Amendment. They really do, except when your point of view is different from theirs! The First Amendment was meant to protect *all* speech, particularly speech that may be unpopular. Of course, when someone says something to liberals that they perceive as offensive, they demand such language be either censored or silenced. It is no secret that liberals go out of their way to find discourse that offends them. Furthermore, liberals go as far as telling others of a particular race or religion that they should be offended by the words of another. Last time I checked, no one in this country was given a right to *not* be offended. On a practical note, it would be impossible for *anybody* to speak if liberals had their way of curtailing all speech that *anyone* could possibly find objectionable.

Labeling certain speech as abhorrent is the instrument liberals use to create victims.

Liberals also use it to leverage power over those who use such supposedly provocative language. For example, if you were to speak out against public policies on *affirmative action* and instead support a system of reward based on the merit of individual action, liberals will immediately accuse you of being filled with hate. This puts the speaker on the defensive, which is a tactic liberals employ to rebuke their enemies into self-imposed silence. Liberals are always demanding public apologies from those who say things publicly that are not in lock step with liberal ideology. When the apology either does not come or is not good enough to liberals' satisfaction, they demand that person be fired from his job. Just ask Don Imus. I thought liberals were the ones always demanding tolerance for diverse views and lifestyles? It must be that liberals are immune to their own dictates.

A standard liberal practice to silence the opposition is the use of the childish maneuver that labels any speech they do not agree with as cruel or mean-spirited. Do you recall as child being called *mean* by another kid for something you said or did? Even if your action was not necessarily malicious, the other kid still accused you of being malicious simply because he did not like your deed. Of course when liberal children grow up and become liberal adults, they many times use a more devious ploy to silence their adversaries. The paragon of all silencing schemes that liberals favor the most is to indict the opposition's speech as *racist*. Liberals relentlessly use the racist claim, even when such a claim is far-fetched, in the hope of damaging their enemies' reputation so as to avoid a real debate on the merits of the argument. Regardless of the advancement in social progress, liberals will endlessly accuse their rivals of having deep-rooted racist beliefs.

When accusations of being mean, hateful, or racist do not work in silencing the competition, liberals use the power of government to get their way. Take for example, hate crime legislation that liberals have unfortunately been successfully able to get passed at both federal and state levels. In the good old days when your average thug attacked or mugged another person, the thug was charged with one or more of the varying degrees of assault and/or robbery. If and when found guilty, the criminal was punished according to the sentencing guidelines for assault, robbery, or other actual crime(s). Today, if the victim belongs to one of the special groups of people liberals proclaim are unduly oppressed – that is anyone who is not a white, heterosexual male – the accused, being prosecuted by a liberal lawyer, may also be convicted with having hateful feelings while committing the *real* crime. So what the liberals are saying is that if, for example, you were to assault a person who happens to be gay, you just might have ill-feelings toward homosexuality. Therefore, according to liberals, your crime may have been solely motivated by hateful, anti-homosexual views. Does that even matter? Isn't most important that the accused *actually* assaulted another, irrespective of what he thinks? What should be judged are not someone's personal beliefs, but his deeds against another. Your line of thinking according to liberals is more important than what you do. Put to its logical conclusion this could mean that while some assaults are committed in hate, others are committed in love! It takes a very imaginative, childish liberal mind to make up this kind of nonsense. Only in the Bizzaro-like world of *Liberalland*, do we try to read peoples' minds and then find them guilty of hating another based on race, religion, or some other artificial label. The bottom line is that liberals not only want to silence what you may say, they also want to prevent you from thinking non-liberal thoughts. Liberals want to make sure you feel shame for thinking in your own way.

Liberal view of the Second Amendment

Liberals do not like the Second Amendment in any way, shape, or form. They try their best to ignore it, pretending that it is not part of the U.S. Constitution. This is because liberals absolutely abhor guns and those who use them. The Second Amendment is simple in its wording: "A well regulated Militia, being necessary to the security of a free State, the right of the people to keep and bear Arms, shall not be infringed." Note that the amendment is composed of two clauses, dependent and independent, respectively. Liberals love to cite the first clause only, as if guns can only be part of the activities related to a state militia. However, the second clause, unlike the first, can stand on its own as a sentence. If you try show a liberal the logic of your argument, he will re-tort with infantile behavior such as labeling you a *gun nut*.

Often times when growing up, scores of children are unfortunately taught to fear guns. Many parents, though with good intensions, ignorantly teach their children to avoid guns at all costs, as if they would be exposed to bubonic plague. It is out of a parental sense of obligation to protect the welfare of their progeny. I myself, was instructed by my parents and school to be afraid of guns. Fortunately as I grew into adulthood, I was able to discover the beneficial aspects of gun ownership. I came to the proper conclusion that a gun is a tool, just like anything else, and it is how it is used that should be judged. Regrettably, liberals do not come to this commonsensical conclusion as adults.

As I stated previously, liberals have the fallacious belief that there are no bad people out there who are willing to hurt others in very violent ways. Young children hold similar views that all people are good. That is why good parenting involves warning children that there are individuals in the world whose sole desire is to harm others. For the few liberals who do acknowledge the existence of criminals, their solution to crime prevention is utterly silly. Liberals lecture that if you are confronted by another who is terrorizing you, you should try to negotiate with that person. Really! So if I just talk to the criminal who is threatening me with bodily harm, often with some kind of weapon, and ask him to stop his behavior, I'll be okay? Only an immature mentality could believe such drivel! Second, liberals have an illogical sense of trepidation for guns the same way youngsters are fearful of the nonexistent *Bogeyman* that they believe is hiding underneath the bed or inside the closet. Do liberals make an effort to learn about guns in order to alleviate the fear? Of course not, that's too difficult! Like electricity, liberals always take the path of least resistance. Third, liberals view objects that they do not like - and guns are probably at the top of their list - as evil, instead of how a person is using that object.

Because liberals live in a magical fairytale land, they take unsound and sometimes downright weird steps in an attempt to steer clear of guns and shun those Americans who own them. The simplest act they endorse with the objective of avoiding firearms is to hang up a sign at the entrance of a building or property banning the possession of any firearm. You've seen them. It's a cute drawing of handgun inside a red circle with diagonal line along with a quip, *No guns allowed on the premises*. You see liberals believe that such signs provide the ultimate in physical protection, similar to how a crucifix or garlic wards off Dracula! This may be because as children we are taught to obey signs. If there is a sign posted, children believe it is iron-clad, immutable, and must be unquestionably carried out. What liberals just cannot grasp is the fact that some children, now and when they grow into adulthood, ignore signs. Liberals falsely believe that if you suspend a sign on the front door prohibiting guns, it will be enthusiastically obeyed by all, including potential criminals. Of course, those of us that live in the real world understand that signs like these only disarm law-abiding citizens and actually make the job of robbery, assault, rape, murder, etc. only easier for would-be lawbreakers. Sometimes these types of signs are codified into law by liberal legislators to produce *gun-free* zones for public schools, universities, and other so-called "sensitive" places. However, the term gun-free zone should realistically be called *unarmed potential victims* zone. I find it fascinating that most of these gun-free areas are in places where liberals amass in great numbers, like institutions of learning.

Liberals are like children when it comes to defense and personal protection; somebody else is responsible for that. Children look to their parents, other adults, or older siblings for protection. In adulthood, liberals do the same by relying exclusively on law enforcement for protection. Just as most children are unable or unwilling to protect themselves during a physical attack, liberals follow suit by refusing to take on any personal responsibility. I find it amusing how rich and famous liberals have no trouble hiring armed personal security teams for themselves and their families, while hypocritically spouting nonsensical talk that there is a critical need to pass laws banning all private ownership of firearms. Most people have heard the phrase, *when seconds count the police are only minutes away.* Of course, when you try to inform liberals that nearly all police responses to crime are after the fact, they reply with some ignoramus remark claiming that if citizens carry guns, ex-police officers will be lining up at the unemployment office.

Obviously, as Americans no one is forced to own or carry a firearm for self-defense. It is an individual choice, which is what America is all about. However, liberals do not want anyone, other than government, to have the choice of possessing and/or carrying a firearm. They do not want you to be able to take on any personal responsibility for your own protection or that of your family. This is because your typical liberal, similar to a child's state of mind, believes that *if I don't have something,* (due to my own free choice)*, you shouldn't have it either.* When you talk to liberals about your lawful right to own and carry guns, as is the case in most U.S. states, they respond by saying that your fear of potential personal harm is irrational. My supposed irrational fear is not anybody's business but mine nor does it harm anyone. Not to mention, who is anyone to tell me that my intuitions on the possibility of harm from others are irrational?

When discussing potential gun laws, liberals always call for *common sense* legislation. Of course, you can never get a liberal to define or list what common sense gun laws should be on the books. This is because what liberals really want is a total ban of all guns, at least those that are privately owned. There are two different lines of thinking within the liberal belief system when it comes to firearms. The first liberal camp is convinced that anyone outside of their distorted belief system is too stupid to own a firearm for any purpose. Much more nefarious than the first, the second camp hates freedom and realizes that private gun ownership impedes their vision of a one-world government under totalitarian rule, something many liberals truly desire. Liberals in government would love to disarm average Americans, but would never entertain the idea of disarming government (Some of the more famous want to be gun-grabbers include: New York City Mayor Michael Bloomberg; U.S. Senators Diane Feinstein and Chuck Schumer; U.S. House Representatives Nancy Pelosi and Bobby Rush). Not to mention, the goal of having an unarmed, defenseless population plays into the liberal craving to make all citizens completely dependent on government, which includes the need for physical protection.

When it is reported in the news that someone walked into school or workplace and began shooting people indiscriminately, liberals cannot find a news media microphone fast enough to demand the enactment of stricter gun laws. If you try to explain to a liberal that the alleged perpetrator already broke multiple federal and state gun laws during the shooting rampage and that no gun law will ever completely prevent future occurrences, you are accused of not caring about innocent people dying. Refusing to accept their anti-gun stance will cause them to accuse you of having blood on your hands, as if you pulled the trigger yourself. News media liberals are disingenuous when it comes to reporting incidents related to firearm use. They enthusiastically report when someone uses a gun to purposely hurt others while omitting news of a citizen using a firearm to defend himself from the attack of a criminal. Liberals, pretending to be journalists, have an agenda and that is to report all firearm use (with the exception of government use) in a negative tone. A lawfully armed citizen defending himself, his family, and his home does not fit the liberal media's agenda to assist liberal lawmakers in trying to systematically ban all personally owned firearms. To put it bluntly, a liberal would rather see his fellow citizen killed by some villain during a criminal act than to hear about how the same citizen successfully thwarted the hostile attack with a firearm. According to liberals, it is better that you be dead than armed!

Liberal view of the Ninth Amendment

The Ninth Amendment is pretty rudimentary: "The enumeration in the Constitution, of certain rights, shall not be construed to deny or disparage others retained by the people." Basically, this says that Americans have additional rights, not listed specifically in the Bill of Rights. Being instinctive, they include things like a right to associate with others of your choosing, a right to determine the direction of your own life, a right to free movement, and etc. The Founding Fathers reasoned that man is meant to live life in freedom. Man's freedom is the result of being granted rights by God. This is many times referred to as *natural rights*. However, liberals generally miss the mark on this concept or will twist the connotation in order to progress their liberal agenda.

Liberals do not believe in the concept of natural rights bestowed by a higher power that most people, regardless of religious belief, refer to as God. This may due to the fact that an unusually large percentage of liberals, when compared to others within the entire political spectrum, are either atheists or agnostics. Due to their strong secular belief, liberals worship government as a substitute to worshiping God. As a result, liberals mistakenly believe that rights are any commodity or service desired that is to be provided by government. What liberals cannot

seem to understand is that rights have several
unique attributes. For example, natural rights
do not obligate or take away anything from one
person in order to be enjoyed by another person.
Because God does not change, natural rights are
immutable and, therefore, can never be taken
away. If government was the author of rights, it
could change them, take away at will, or use as a
weapon to coerce certain action or behavior from
its citizens. Children gain their understanding
of rights from the types of behaviors their
parents permit them to engage in, as well as the
kind of items they are allowed to possess. A set
of parents, for example, may at some point give
their child a bicycle or pay the freight for him
to participate in a sport or other youth
activity. Without a proper appreciation for the
goods and services a child receives from his
parents and an understanding of what it takes for
them to be able provide those things, that child
will consider such as *entitlements*. When that
same child reaches physical adulthood as a
liberal, he mistaken believes he has a right to
the things he wants, irrespective of who is doing
the provision. Therefore as an adult, the
liberal looks to the government as the provider
of needs and wants just as he looked to his

parents as a child. Furthermore, liberals try
desperately to distort the true definition of
rights to justify obtaining goods and services at
the expense of others. For instance, liberals
continually attempt to classify basic human
needs, such as food, shelter, health care, and
education as rights. In truth, a *right* empowers
an individual to pursue certain activities or
guarantees him protection and a standard set of
procedures that must be followed if accused of a
crime by the government. However, liberals have
convoluted the definition of a right to mean the
provision of products and services. What
liberals never seem to understand is that a right
neither obligates nor burdens one person to
provide something to another. You cannot label
anything a right if it is forced to be produced
or provided by someone else. If you try to
explain this to a liberal, he will begin to
hyperventilate in a similar manner to an overly
excited preschooler on a sugar high. Liberals
will then retort with emotional anecdotes of
hungry and homeless people needing assistance.
However, someone demanding food, shelter, or
something else just because he needs or wants it
means that another person would be required to
provide such things, either voluntarily or by

force. On the contrary, classic rights such as
life, liberty, and the pursuit of happiness, as
stated in the Declaration of Independence do not
impose on *person A* to provide something so that
it can be exercised or enjoyed by *person B*.
Other rights listed in the Bill of Rights, such
as freedom of religious exercise, freedom of
speech, and bearing arms also do not obligate one
to supply in order to be exercised by another.
Given a choice, liberals would prefer to have
free "stuff" over freedom.

Liberal view of the Tenth Amendment

I have yet to come across a liberal who
understands the Tenth Amendment, which states:
"The powers not delegated to the United States by
the Constitution, nor prohibited by it to the
States, are reserved to the States respectively,
or to the people." Simply stated, whatever
powers are not granted to the federal government
nor restricted from the states by the
Constitution are the prerogative of the
individual states and its people. Therefore,
notwithstanding specific constitution prohibition
(coin money, declare war, etc.) states are free
to make their own laws. Generally understood as

exclusive domain, it is one of the basic principles of federalism. When the Constitution was amended to include the Bill of Rights, those rights only applied to the relationship between the federal government and its citizens. However over the years, the Supreme Court and other inferior courts have gradually ruled that specified rights within the Bill of Rights apply to the states as well. This is commonly referred to as *incorporation*. Today, almost all of the rights within the Bill of Rights have been incorporated against the states through the *due process* clause listed in the Fourteenth Amendment.

Some folks argue that incorporation of the Bill of Rights was not the original intent of the Fourteenth Amendment. Furthermore, the Founding Fathers' intention was to give the states the right to draft their own list of citizens' rights, if they chose to do so through the Tenth Amendment. I am not going to argue at this time on whether or not incorporation is proper or constitutional. What I am going to articulate is that liberals only advocate this amendment when it suits them. Either, we follow a strict Tenth Amendment constitutional interpretation or we follow an incorporation interpretation. For example, I'm sure liberals in the media believe fully in the incorporation of the *freedom of the press* clause of the First Amendment and most other parts of the Bill of Rights. Just like a child who changes the rules of a game while it is being played, liberals fall back to a Tenth Amendment constitutional interpretation only when it matches their liberal ideology, such as to deny Second Amendment rights to citizens at a state level. When it comes to gun rights, liberals will claim a Tenth Amendment right for a state to harshly regulate or prohibit firearm possession and use. For most other issues, liberals resort back to an incorporation view.

Chapter 3: Liberals and their liberal causes

Liberals are always championing causes. Since they generally are not rooted with a spiritual connection to God, liberals are continually moving from one cause to another in a futile attempt to fill a void within themselves that is produced from not having such a relationship, as well as to find purpose and meaning for their lives. Regardless of how inane the topic at hand, there is always some liberal pointing out that *this* or *that* is in dire straits unless we immediately act. This is because liberals have a distorted, grandiose view of their importance to correcting the ills of the world. However, the actual *cause du jour* liberals cry about is not nearly as important as is the appearance to others that liberals *care* about the issue. Liberals have an insatiable need to find inequity and injustice, whether real or imaginary, in order to show others that they are overflowing with concern and compassion. Because liberals are unfulfilled in their own lives, they feel a need to take on some kind of cause in order to draw the attention of others, similar to how a child persistently shows off his talents or accomplishments to parents, siblings, and peers.

Even when liberals are genuinely sincere about a cause, the public's perception of *their caring* always outweighs the viability of potential solutions for alleviating the problem. In other words, actually solving a dilemma takes a back seat to the liberals' need to boast their concern to others. The remedies that liberals offer, which have often been proven through repeated experience to not work, are always the same. Generally, liberals only give two choices, create more laws/regulations or doll out more public money, all at the expense of individual liberty.

The number one means that liberals employ to attract public attention to their cause of the moment is a public boycott. When normal people are dissatisfied with the service, quality of products, or the business practices of a company or sole proprietor, they privately boycott those entities. Liberals on the other hand, who continuously crave attention like a child having an emotion outburst in an attempt to play on the sympathies of his parents, make a public spectacle of their boycotts. In conjunction with a boycott, liberals also like to mix in a highly publicized demonstration march (Amazing how you often times see Reverends Jesse Jackson and Al Sharpton leading these marches!). Irrespective of whether or not there is enough local outrage to support a public boycott or demonstration, liberals will pay people, even those who have no concern or connection to the issue, to show up at a protest site. Many times liberals call upon labor unions to invoke their members to participate. It is also common practice for liberals to bus people in from other locations, in order to create a false perception of the scope of public outrage. Of course no boycott or demonstration would be complete without the full support and cooperation of liberal media coverage, which is more than happy to use its powerful and far-reaching medium to promote the liberal cause.

If all else fails to attract enough public interest necessary to enact the legislative change liberals want for their cause, they will resort to filing frivolous lawsuits. When liberals do not get their way at the ballot box or through the legislative process, like a young child screaming because dad would not buy him a particular toy at the store, they petition for judicial intervention, the same way the child would plead to mom for relief. Liberals have no qualms with subverting the rule of law for their purposes. Not long ago, the state of California put *Proposition 8* on the ballot to amend its constitution. It was a referendum that said "only marriage between a man and a woman is valid or recognized in California". Of course when liberals did not win the majority vote as they had expected, they sued. Aren't liberals always broadcasting how wonderful democracy is? I guess they only like democracy when it advances their causes.

Liberal view of voting

The liberal motto when it comes to voting is *vote early, vote often*. Because liberals cannot win in the arena of ideas, they have to make sure liberal politicians obtain elected office by any means available, including outright voter fraud. Liberals have no trouble being dishonest in order to get what they want, the same way they did as children, cheating on their schoolwork. In order to ensure fraud takes place under the guise of fairness and equal access to the democratic process, liberals unabashedly support the repealing of individual state laws that require citizens to present some form of government-issued photo identification before being allowed to vote, decrying that such a requirement

disenfranchise voters. You see, liberals believe
no one should be required to prove who he says he
is before accessing the voting booth. Ensuring
the integrity of the election process means very
little to liberals. Of course, the so-called
disenfranchisement claim only applies to certain
individuals that liberals classify into specific
groups, generally along racial demographics (I
talk about this in greater detail later in the
book). Also, such stipulations, according to
liberals, put an undue burden on certain groups
of voters. Their bogus allegation is that many
people in these groups do not possess any type of
government-issued identification and obtaining
such would be an unbearable financial
encumbrance. What I would like to know is how do
such people, living in the shadows, as liberals
love to argue, conduct their everyday activities
without identification? For instance, it is the
policy of many housing complexes for perspective
tenants to produce valid identification before
they will be allowed to view a vacant apartment
for rent. Even when state law asserts that
citizens lacking proper identification will be
provided it for free if they cannot afford the
cost themselves, liberals still cry foul. Free
IDs paid for by the taxpayers are not good enough

35

for liberals. For just about everything, liberals want free of charge, but not ID!

Likewise, liberals also do not like the requirement that a potential voter provide a proper address when registering. It is not unheard for liberals to retain lawyers to challenge in court residency requirement laws in order to allow vagrants to vote using the name of a particular park as an address. You see requiring identification and valid addresses means that liberals would not be able to get their minions bused to multiple polling districts so they can vote often. In plain English it is purposely getting individuals on a mass scale, to vote multiple times in the same election. Didn't liberals in Sixties fighting for the passage of the Voting Rights Act exclaim, *one man, one vote*? Not to mention, isn't responsible action on the part of each citizen a prerequisite to maintaining a functioning free society? Leave it to a liberal to make sure that those who are not U.S. citizens get to have a say in the voting booth.

I am sure most reading this either recollect or have read about the debacle in Florida following the 2000 Presidential Election. Because the Electoral College count was so close and the percentage of popular votes in Florida separating the two main candidates was less than one tenth of 1%, liberals sprung into action to try to make sure their candidate won the state, irrespective of the true vote count. How did they do this you may ask? First, liberals demanded that only the votes of certain counties, those heavily populated with liberal voters, be recounted. Second, even though the infamous "butterfly" ballot had been in use in Florida elections for years, liberals all of a sudden made absurd contentions that the ballot's format confused voters into choosing a candidate they did not intend to pick. Third, many liberals actually had the audacity to demand for a new election. I am sure a re-election would have been free of fraud and corruption! Fourth, liberals injected racism into the debate by claiming that police and private entities suppressed minority voter turnout through various intimidation tactics. Lastly, after automated recounts still did not push their candidate ahead, liberals filed lawsuits (something liberals are good at) in an attempt to prevent the state from certifying its election results and demand that only *cherry-picked* counties conduct manual hand recounts. During the fiasco, barely a day went by without hearing a liberal demand we forego the constitutional requirement of the Electoral College and simply go by plurality of the national vote total. I must say, liberals really do have respect for the rule of law, as long as the law supports their rules.

Liberal view of immigration

There is a line in the John Lennon song *Imagine* that goes: "Imagine there's no countries. It isn't hard to do." This is the liberal fairytale dream. They desire a world where there are no differences. While in school, several generations of children have been brainwashed by liberals to believe that all cultures are on equal footing and that everyone can live together in complete harmony. Liberals probably have a longing for their kindergarten days when the teacher would have all the pupils sit in a circle to sing the Disney song, *It's a Small World*. Recalling memories of the repeated chorus phrase, "It's a small world after all", probably gives these liberals goose bumps! However, the hard truth that liberals cannot seem to swallow is that nations and borders are set up because various groups of people throughout the world have radically different cultures, beliefs and lifestyles. These differences are largely based on religious convictions. The concept of the *nation-state* was firmly established after the *Peace of Westphalia* in the 17th Century. Despite this, liberals still fantasize about a united world where no borders exist. Once achieved, liberals fallaciously believe that everyone will live in a permanent state of peace. Of course the only way to attain such a world would be to force everyone on the planet into one culture, one religion, and one belief system, not something that can be attained through peaceful means.

To help pave the way toward this lofty goal, liberals consistently trample upon the concept of national sovereignty. Unabashed support of illegal immigration is a favorite choice among liberals to achieve this objective. Liberals believe that any foreigner should be allowed into the United States for any reason, irrespective of the law. When you explain to a liberal that it is essential to the survival of any civil society to maintain respect for the rule of law, you will get juvenile anecdotes of poor immigrant people just trying to make a better life for themselves. However, no nation can maintain its freedom or sovereignty if any foreigner can come into the country, at any time for any reason.

Liberals use several methods to assist illegal aliens to stay in the country. As mentioned earlier in this writing, a highly publicized protest is the liberals' favorite tactic. Gathering at pro-immigration rallies, liberals seek to play on the sympathies of the public with violin-worthy tales of how current immigration laws are separating families. This is done in an effort to obtain public outrage, hoping large numbers of citizens will petition Congress to ease or revoke current immigration laws. I have to laugh when liberal celebrities protest at these rallies and, afterwards, jet set back to their secluded and gated neighborhoods (It's beneath a liberal to actual live among *common* men). Second, liberals will overtly refuse to obey current immigration law. Since the rule of law equates to nothing for your average liberal, those in charge of local governments have no trouble rebuking federal law by enacting sanctuary ordinances that prohibit local law enforcement from reporting known illegal aliens to federal authorities; hence, we get the term *sanctuary city*. Third, liberals will use an alternate term to hide the dilemma and mask the true nature of the illegal immigration. For example, the term *illegal alien* suddenly becomes *undocumented worker*. You see, liberals want you to believe that every person who treks illegally into the United States does so solely to seek employment, and that such individuals just forgot to stop at the border to fill out the proper paperwork. If you do not buy into their spin, liberals will label you as a racist, just like they do when you exercise free speech. To add insult to injury, they profess that immigrants fill manual labor jobs that Americans just refuse to take. Though many do come here for employment with the prospect of higher wages, a large number also come here for nefarious purposes such as drug smuggling, sex trafficking, and other crimes. Not to mention, lax immigration enforcement puts the United States at risk for acts of terrorism. Even if the *Liberalland* notion that all illegal immigration is exclusively to seek a better life, liberals refuse to grasp the harsh economic reality that unrestrained immigration leads to depressed wages for American citizens, and an overbearing drain on financial resources and community infrastructures, such as schools, hospitals, and social services. I wonder why you never see a

41

liberal offer to take an "undocumented worker" into his home? I can't wait for the day when I see liberals begin to line up in droves to sponsor these poor, helpless people just wanting a chance to experience American life.

Liberal view of education

Education is a powerful but sensitive subject for liberals. This is because liberals commonly default to it when debating any topic, even if the topic at hand has nothing to do with education. They use education to stir up emotions and to mask their ignorance of other matters. Whether you are talking to liberals about tax policy, the job market, or national defense, they inevitably change the subject to education. Plus, liberals love to add children into the mix, a large component of education. If you disagree with liberals on increasing education funding or higher pay for teachers, you are accused of having contempt for children.

Most of us growing up viewed our school teachers as flawless beings who were paragons of virtue and wisdom. Of course, as we grew up, most of us began to realize that teachers are just as fallible as the rest of us. Just look at all school teachers in the news in recent years that have been charged and convicted of having sex or other inappropriate relationships with their students. Liberals look to public school teachers as the high priests and priestesses for advancing the liberal gospel. As such, liberals always paint public school teachers as the most pious among us in society, as well as overworked and underpaid. God forbid if you ever suggest to a liberal that some people become teachers strictly out of a desire of wanting a secure, tenured job that features regular hours and lots of holidays and vacation periods. In other terms, some individuals become teachers more so for selfish reasons than a desire to educate children.

Liberals understand very well that children are the future. Of course, liberals want to control that future and therefore advocate that the education of children is something only government can accomplish. The liberal playbook for controlling education consists of two strategies. First, over the last several decades liberal educators have conveyed to their students the narcissistic notion that everyone is *special*; everyone deserves an award just for showing up. What I would like a liberal to tell me is, if everyone is special, who is average? Second, liberals endeavor to "dumb" down education standards, so that no one feels left out or excluded. Leave it to a liberal to decrease quality standards to the lowest common denominator. By doing so, liberals hold back brighter students so as to not offend the slower ones. Liberals never forgot those awful childhood feelings they experienced when they were called upon by the teacher to answer a question, but because they didn't study were unable to respond! Because liberals only want certain ideas taught to children, government monopoly of education is a sure means to guarantee only liberal ideology is taught (I wonder how we were ever able to educate children before the 1979 creation of the Department of Education?). It is no wonder liberals are hostile toward the idea of parents home-schooling their own children. Even though liberals always like to profess how great the public school system is, those liberals who can afford to do so, often send their kids to private schools. Could it be that some liberals realize that in comparison to public schools, private schools often better educate students at half the cost?

When it comes to higher education, liberals believe that it ought to be a right provided free of charge by government. In other words, somebody else needs to foot the bill. Again, liberals are attempting to turn a commodity into an entitlement. Young liberal college students do not mind taking out exorbitant student loans so they can attend very expensive private universities, in order to take non-world relevant majors like *Women's Studies* or *18th Century Poetry*. However, they never complain about the schools that are actually responsible for jacking up tuition rates year after year. Instead, they blame the loaning institutions that lent them money for their education and even have the gall to demand those loans be reduced or forgiven. As if loan officers across the country held a gun to the heads of students, forcing them into these loans. It is hilarious how liberals allege that "big oil", "big pharmaceutical", or "big retail" is constantly raking the public over the coals. On the other hand, you hear nothing but crickets in response to suggesting the possibility of "big education" engaging in questionable business practices.

Is it not odd that an overwhelming majority of university professors fall into the liberal column of political thought? It makes you wonder if the saying, *those who can't do, teach,* has a ring of truth to it. Because liberals view education as something that should be provided to all free of cost, I wonder why you never see a liberal professor offer to teach pro bono?

Liberal view of health care

Just like education, liberals consider the provision of health care as a right. Liberals probable hold this belief due to childhood nostalgia. We all recall skinning our knees and elbows at one time or another as kids. Those of us who were fortunate enough to have a stable home life could always run home to have our booboos tended to by a loving mother. After a thorough cleaning of the wound, a good mother would blow a kiss on it to make it better, - yes we all know about germs - put a bandage on it, give a huge hug, and send her child back outside to play. Liberals look at all health care as uncomplicated as a mother always ready with a bandage and hug. Of course in the adult world, health care is not that simplistic.

Given the liberals' child-like approach to life, it is understandable that they cannot bear to see pain and suffering in others. However, the liberal solution of free health care provision to all is not only unrealistic but actually detrimental to the overall liberties we still hold in this country. It is easy to say that everyone should be provided health care, while actually delivering it is a whole different issue. What liberals fail to understand is, that in order for someone to receive health care service, another person or groups of persons must either be willing or forced to provide it. That is where the liberal daydream hits a brick wall. Whether it is the need for food, shelter, clothing, or health care, needs are fulfilled through private transactions involving at least two parties commonly known as purchases. However, for liberals to emphatically demand that *person A* be provided health care services, would mean that either *person B* (doctor/health care provider) or *person C* (taxpayer) is obligated to provide something to *person A* without just compensation. Since it is outside the scope of human nature for people to be completely altruistic means that either the health care provider is forced by the hand of government to provide his services free of charge to a designated beneficiary, or the taxpayer is forced to provide money that pays for the beneficiary to obtain health care services. This line of thinking could logically be applied to anything else, which would mean that any need *person A* may have is to be provided by *person B* and/or *person C* without regard to *B* and *C's* labor or pecuniary costs. Nowhere in this equation is *person A* required to contribute anything towards his own needs. Therefore, it would only be rational for *persons B* and *C* to refuse to contribute their time and labor and just wait around for someone else, maybe *person D*, to provide them something for nothing. However, making health care or any other commodity a "right" within the law gives government the power to use force if necessary to ensure those commodities are provided as dictated. Government having the power to force a citizen to give up his labor or property for the benefit of another is the definition of tyranny, which is the polar opposite of American liberty. Once government has the power to compel one citizen to use his labor and/or property so that health care can be provided to another, it also will have the power to determine which citizens are entitled to health care services and which are denied the same.

Liberal view of the environment

Like children, liberals become very upset when they are reminded that some things in the world are beyond man's control, such as the weather and the environment in general. The liberal consensus is that human beings are destroying the planet, simply by our existence. Their false predictions of what life on Earth will be like in 10, 50, or 100 years is always described in catastrophic terms. Of course liberals have warned for decades that if mankind does not stop doing this or start to changes its ways, the world will burn up. None of their dire predictions ever come to pass. A favorite argument for liberals is the old, *the science is settled*, malarkey. If anyone disagrees, liberals go on the attack with juvenile name-calling like *flat earther*. We in the know, realize that liberals' true goal is to control and ultimately destroy the economic freedom of all Americans, under the guise of *saving* the planet. Curtailing economic freedom is what liberals hope to accomplish so as to one day enslave people into a one-world government.

The primary reason most liberals are overly zealous about environmental protection is because

the Earth, the environment, and its eco-systems
are their gods, in a sense mimicking the
Christian belief of the Father, Son, and Holy
Spirit. As I mentioned early in this book, it is
well established that many liberals hold either
atheistic or agnostic points of view. However,
regardless of one's religious views, we are all
created with an inborn need to be connected with
our Creator. Liberals attempt to heed to this
necessity by merely replacing reverence for the
Creator with reverence for creation. Therefore,
this radical belief system on environmentalism
becomes a religion for liberals. Attempting to
debunk the myths of environmental calamity with a
liberal is considered blasphemous. Since all
religions need followers in order to survive and
thrive, liberals do their best to attract new
disciples by way of propaganda. Through the use
scary language and premonitions, liberals have
been successful in attracting new followers and
offering false hopes of personal *salvation*
through good acts toward the environment.

Initially, liberals warned us about *global
warming*. When that term no longer fitted the
reality that median world temperatures have
dropped in recent years, liberals switched to
global climate change. In addition to these

scare tactics, liberals also tell you that following their dictates in relation to the environment will be a *friendly* or *responsible* action. Not too long ago, many manufactures began labeling their products, everything from laundry detergent to copier paper as *environmentally friendly*. I am sure that companies' good marketing schemes and the desire to attract new customers based on popular culture trends had nothing to do with the placement of such labels, but I digress. Therefore, by choosing the environmentally friendly stamped product over one that is not, liberals are trying to convince you that your choice results in being friendly toward the environment. Of course, when liberals believe not enough people are making the *correct* consumer product choice, they use guilt to persuade you that you are being irresponsible. Hence, the environmentally friendly label on a multitude of products has slowly evolved to *environmentally responsible*. Therefore, if you were to choose the product that does not have the environmentally responsible tag over the one that does, according to liberals, you would be acting irresponsibly.

Likewise, *carbon footprint* is another term liberals use, that they created out of thin air, in order to make people feel remorse over their own existence (Keep in mind, liberals hate their lives and want you to hate yours as well!). With this term, liberals look at all the resources an individual consumes during a defined period or an entire lifetime and then calculates the amount of carbon "pollution" one's existence has been left for the planet to deal with. For example, liberals will look at the amount of gasoline the average American consumes during a lifetime of travel via privately owned vehicles and then calculates how much pollution was emitted into the environment from the burnt fuel. Liberals then try to create anxiety in people by telling them the planet is getting hotter because excess carbon dioxide in the atmosphere is trapping heat from sun. After trying their best to make you feel guilty, liberals then offer you "penance" for your "sins" of supposedly excessive fuel consumption through such ploys as planting extra trees, participating in *carbon trading*, or your promise to use more public transportation. I thought carbon was one of the most abundant natural elements on the planet? Don't plants thrive on carbon dioxide? Does this mean that such an innocuous act as breathing is detrimental to the environment? A child who does not get his way will threaten to hold his breath until the situation changes to his satisfaction. I think liberals would like us all to hold our breath. Since liberals declare that carbon dioxide is so damaging to the planet, then I think we should encourage them to hold their breath for as long as possible.

Liberals scorn oil and incessantly warn that there is an immediate need to switch to alternative forms of energy. Their hatred of oil has more to do with its unattractive visual and odorous properties, than the fact that it is a potent source of energy, as well as relatively cheap and very reliable. If mankind did not use this powerful energy resource, as liberals wish, the oil would just sit in the ground doing nothing. That would be like not having shelter while being surrounded by numerous trees and refusing to cut some down to build houses. However, you can never convince a liberal that oil, in conjunction with the internal combustion engine, was a primary catalyst responsible for elevating the standard of living exponentially for untold millions of people over the last few generations. Oil fuels the engine of freedom and prosperity. It has provided the means for mass numbers of people to travel frequently and inexpensively throughout the world, thus, spurring commerce. Not to mention, oil is used by various industries in the manufacture of all sorts of consumer goods that all people use on a daily basis, such as plastics. The alternatives to oil and other fossil fuels like coal, according to liberals, are natural sources such as wind and solar. Of course fossil fuels are just as natural and organic as anything else the liberals tell us we should be using. Try telling a liberal that currently neither wind nor solar power can get an airplane off the ground and you will hear him whine like a baby. Their resistance to accepting this fact could be due to recalling past memories of making paper airplanes during their youth. They never forgot the joy they experienced seeing their homemade paper planes float on the air and being propelled by the wind. It must be that the simple liberal mind is convinced that real aircraft should able to run on wind power just as well as the paper ones do.

Liberals do not lead by example. They dictate to others how to live, while doing the opposite in their own lives. For example, liberal politicians and celebrities constantly reprimand the rest of us for not cutting down our use of fossil fuels by foregoing personnel conveyance for public transportation, while hypocritically using private or charted aircraft for themselves. Also, it should be no surprise that liberals love to show off to others how much they care about whatever liberal environmental cause of the month they are spouting about. Most liberals who drive a hybrid car – and there is nothing wrong with driving a hybrid, if you believe it is the best car for you – do so, not so much because they think it will lessen any supposed *environmental impact*, but to demonstrate to others that they care. They tell the American people that we all need to switch to electric powered vehicles. Yet, liberals do not comprehend the fact that a good portion of electricity in the United States is generated through the burning of fossil fuels. Under the liberals' plan, instead of "greenhouse gases" being released into the atmosphere from the cars on the highway, it would be released at power plant as the fossil-fuel is converted into electricity. According to liberals, that's progress!

Attempting to debate them on the merits of the argument will generally result in liberals experiencing fits of rage. For example, liberals get very upset when you tell them that the Ice

Age and other warming and cooling periods
throughout the Earth's billions of years of
existence came about all without the benefit of a
fossil-fueled Industrial Age, or the internal
combustion engine. Liberals profess that mankind
is causing weather changes, but can never answer
why we cannot make it rain in places we would
like it to or rid ourselves of bitterly cold
winters. Personally, I would like to see
Antarctica transformed into a beach-goers'
paradise! If mankind is the cause of hurricanes,
tornadoes, flooding, and other unfavorable
weather activities, wouldn't it make sense that
we would be able to control and direct these
activities? These liberal environmental
worshippers probably were never able to get
passed horrible childhood memories of the
disappointment they felt when a picnic or
ballgame was interrupted by a thunderstorm!

Chapter 4:   Liberal view of American principles

There are certain principles that are unique to America. Principles such as respect and reverence for capitalism, private property, and individualism are some of the reasons the United States has experienced unrestrained prosperity in its relatively short history, when compared to other countries that have been in existence for much longer. However, liberals despise these principles, which is probably why they continually champion the idea that America should be restructured to mirror the quasi-socialist countries of Europe. It is no secret that liberals have absolute contempt for America as it was founded. Make no mistake, even though these self-proclaimed elites label themselves as *liberals*, individual *liberty* is not something they advocate for the masses. Their objective is radical egalitarianism. Therefore, liberals see it necessary to trash these principles in order to condition people to believe that government should and can make everyone equal in all aspect of life. Of course their goal of universal equality does not mean a rise in everybody's standard of living, just the polar opposite. As it is with children, liberals do not like high standards; it's too exclusive and thus unfair!

Liberal view of capitalism

Despite the derision from many, in truthfulness capitalism has lifted millions of individuals out of poverty, more than any and all other political structures put together. Deep down inside, liberals are jealous of anyone that is successful in life, which may be due to the continuous losing streaks they experienced in their youth while playing *Monopoly*. Hence, capitalism is an anathema to liberals. Liberals believe that a system where individuals *voluntarily engage in mutually beneficial exchanges* is downright cruel. They incessantly decry that capitalism is unfair, because it produces unequal outcomes. This is because liberals hate the fact that such a system exists where *anyone* (including themselves) can become wealthy through their own hard work and offers *everyone* the opportunity of economic mobility. What liberals refuse to acknowledge is that before capitalism the overwhelming majority of the world's population, from all previous generations, lived in utter squalor and continually struggled just to survive from day to day. Many were unsure when and where they would obtain their next meal. Not to mention, life expectancy pre-capitalism was half of what is today. Calling capitalism unjust is the means liberals use to conceal their own slothfulness. Can you hark back to your childhood days to that one fellow classmate in school that use to always ask if he could copy your homework or glance over your shoulder during a test? If you refused, the classmate, who eventually grew up to become a liberal, would complain it was unfair that you would receive a better grade than him.

Because liberals like to take the easy way out, they demand that the United States move in a socialist direction, some even calling for an all out communist system. This was evident during the recent *Occupy Wall Street* protests, when demonstrators demanded free stuff from the 1% richest in the country and alleged that this minority is oppressing the masses. The protesters, largely made up of supposedly educated college graduates (Consider, most of these individuals attended very liberal universities), marched in demonstrations demanding for radical equality of wealth through higher tax rates and other re-distributive ruses. If a rich individual, a "one percenter", was to protest against incessant tax increases, liberals will accuse him of being selfish. What does it really mean to be selfish? Who is actually selfish, the individual who wants to keep what he *earned* or the person demanding that free goods and services be provided to him by another? Liberals consider anyone (except their favorite liberal politicians, performing artists, and sports figures) who has more money than they do as greedy. In their distorted view, to be poor is virtuous, honorable, and good, while being rich is mean, cruel, and evil. In other words, if you live in poverty, you are living an honorable and moral life, but if you are wealthy or desire to become so, you are a wretched and wicked person. So let's all live a life of poverty, so that we can be worthy in the eyes of a liberal! Sorry, but I refuse to follow suit.

Not surprising, liberals either will not or cannot comprehend real-world economic concepts. Liberals love to paint the word *profit* as something to be scorned. In reality, when an entrepreneur, through his own hard work and determination decides to start a business with the main goal of earning profit, he *hires* other people to assist in growing such business. Those new hires now earn income, which they did not

have before, to do with as they please. Through
hard work and determination of their own, these
employees have the opportunity to someday
themselves become employers, who intern, will
hire other people to help them make profits.
Thus begins a continuous cycle.

Even when wealthy individuals do not directly
employ others through a business, they indirectly
provide employment to unseen thousands of people
through their purchases and affluent lifestyles.
Since rich people generally can afford to
purchase multiple homes and vehicles, as well as
engage in elaborate travel and other eclectic
activities, their demand for these products and
services results in the employment of others to
meet those needs.

I have never met anyone who obtained job from a
poor man. The exception to the rule would be
liberal politicians, who use the indigent as a
means to stay in elected office. By continuing
to pass wealth re-distribution programs at all
levels of government, liberals actual hurt the
poor by enabling them to become dependent on
government programs. Hence, impoverished
individuals are coaxed to continually vote for
the politicians - the overwhelming majority being
liberals - who promise the most "freebies" from

the public coffers. This leaves the poor exactly where they are, with little or no chance of social mobility. It is this type of liberal ideology and policies that wrongfully lead many to conclude that capitalism is the culprit.

What liberals never understand is that only capitalism can and has produced the products, services, technical advances, and conveniences that they and everyone else outside of *Liberalland* enjoy. For instance, there has never been a socialist or communist nation that has invented, created, or produced anything in comparison to Coca-Cola, cell phones, the Internet, or polio vaccine, just to name a few. One the other hand, communism has always been the leader in producing starvation, poverty, mass murder, disease, and incessant wars. While capitalism's greatest contribution to the world has been universal opportunity for a better lifestyle to those living under such systems, communism's number one contribution has been universal despair for all, except for the 1% that control the system. The real difference between the two political systems is that under capitalism, *everybody*, through cultivation and application of individual talents, has the same opportunity to be in the 1%, whereas under communism you can only join the 1% through either birth or corruption.

Liberal view of private property

Remember when you were little and brought something special of yours into school for *show and tell*? Do you also recall the school bully who tried to either take or break your property after seeing it? Liberals are just like those school bullies you prefer to forget. They do not respect the property of others. This is because liberals do not believe in the concept of private property. Instead, they espouse the idea that everything in the world should be owned collectively, where government will equally parcel out the things it determines its citizens should have. Jealously and envy of what others have is the true reason liberals would like to ban individual ownership. Liberals falsely believe that parity of property will bring about total bliss, when in reality it can produce only uniform misery. To achieve this goal, liberals do everything in their power to *grant* property to those they feel are deserving. However, liberals will not admit that in order give one party some type of property it must first be taken away from another party backed by the full force of government.

Liberal attorneys and politicians many times argue that there is no such thing as private property. One of the ways in which liberals try to erode private property rights is through the practice of *eminent domain*, where privately owned land can be seized by government, upon the provision of just financial compensation to the owner, for legitimate public needs such as the construction of a new highway. However, liberals in government have abused eminent domain in order to increase government coffers. Under the guise of public need, there have been times when liberals wrongly seized private property from one entity, only to sell it to another entity or group who promises to improve the property with businesses, such as a strip mall. The property then becomes more valuable and will yield more tax revenue. Imposing eminent domain is solely for the purpose of acquiring private property on the basis of its unique location as it relates to a valid public need, not to raise more public money for liberal politicians to doll out to their allies!

Liberals also attempt to steal private property from others through excessive taxation. A day never goes by without hearing a liberal demand that the government increase the tax rates on those who earn more than some magical dollar figure. Of course, that figure varies greatly depending on which liberal is speaking at the moment or what audience is being addressed at the time. Also, a liberal will never admit that, due to the voluminous number of credits and deductions that are embedded into the tax code, a large portion of the working U.S. population do not end up paying federal taxes. Many even receive tax refunds that are larger than what was withheld from their paychecks throughout the year. However, liberals ceaselessly petition those still paying taxes to fork over more, demanding everyone pay their *fair share*. If you protest high tax rates, liberals will endeavor to make you feel guilty by accusing you of having contempt for the underprivileged. Not surprising, liberals never define what percentage of income in taxes they consider to be fair. Make no mistake; liberals would tax all, but their cronies, at a 100% rate if they could do so without causing mass riots.

Of course, federal and state tax codes are not the only tool that liberals use to rob others of personal property. Particularly at the local level of government, liberal politicians love to add little hidden taxes or fees in order to generate revenue, such as requiring its citizens to acquire and pay for permits or licenses in order to engage in certain practices or fields of employment. Other times liberals enact local ordinances to both limit the number of people engaging in specific activities and raise revenue. For example, in areas of the country where firearm ownership, particularly handguns, is not popular with local officials (New York City, Washington D.C., Chicago), liberals in government ratify local laws to severely limit access. On top of imposing extremely onerous permit processes designed to discourage ordinary citizens from attempting to legally acquire a firearm, liberals also impose exorbitant fees in order fill the local treasury. As a result, only the privileged few who have the connections and the money can obtain such permits.

Lastly, liberals fancy on charging bloated fines and imposing ridiculous court fees in order to resolve simple infractions such as a parking ticket. I remember a few years ago getting pulled over by a local sheriff deputy while driving home from work. The officer cited me for failing to obey a highway sign. Acknowledging guilt, I signed the ticket and mailed it to the county court, along with my fine. If memory serves me right, the fine was $30. However, there was a court fee of $61, more than twice the fine. It perplexed me why the court fee was so high. Since I mailed in the ticket, I did not take up the court's time or resources by showing up in person and demanding a trial, which would have been my right to do so. Bottom line is that liberals have rackets like this in place to siphon extra money from people so it can be used for some hare-brained liberal program. Liberals adore spending other people's money!

Liberal view of individualism

Liberals experience nausea when anyone promotes the idea of the uniquely American founding principle known has individualism. This is due to the reprehensible liberal belief that all people are part of a collective, where the individual's existence is solely for that benefit. Since liberals find everything unfair, the collective mindset is their means to make up for either laziness or personal short comings that they are unwilling to accept. Because liberals are constantly demanding handouts, individuals are only important to liberals as far as what is believed they can provide to the collective. Individuals are expendable in the advancement of the liberal agenda, which is increased political power for the self-righteous liberal class and more government regulation and intervention into the lives of all Americans.

In order to destroy individuality, liberals endeavor to diminish the dignity we all possess as uniquely created individuals. They do this primarily by classifying all people into various groups using demographics such as ethnicity, religion, and gender. Liberals then designate characteristics to all within each group such as political party affiliation, education level, income earning potential, and social beliefs. God forbid if someone, being an individual first, believes or acts in contrary to the liberals' designated characteristics! Not only that, liberals also assume certain injustices have been suffered by all persons within some of these groups, such as job discrimination or racial intolerance. You see liberals deny the reality that all people are born with distinctive traits, aptitudes, and talents. As far as liberals are concerned, people might as well be bricks. Bricks in a wall are uniform. If a brick becomes cracked or broken, you pull it out and replace with a new one. This is how liberals view people. If someone is not doing as instructed or promoting the liberal agenda, the group will replace and dispose of that person in a heartbeat. Liberals always claim to be fighting for the rights of minorities. However, they deny rights to the smallest minority there is, the minority of the individual.

Why do liberals classify all individuals into groups you may ask? The painful truth is that liberals do this so they can label victimhood to certain people for their own self-serving purposes. (Victims equal potential liberal voters!). Once liberals assign you to one of their groups, they do their best to convince you of one of two different storylines. Either you have been getting the shaft, the short end of the stick your whole life or you have been the cause of the injustices suffered by others. Therefore, you either need relief from these injustices that you have endured, or you are the root of the problem and need to pay for your indiscretions. Furthermore, liberals lie through their teeth – like a young child with crumbs around his mouth, who denies to his parents that he just had his hands in the cookie jar – by telling the alleged victim that they are the only ones who can reverse the injustices he has suffered. Liberals do this to gain political power for themselves. You see to liberals, you, the individual, are no different than a lab animal in an experiment. The individual is merely a means to an end for liberal progression.

Because of their disgust for human life, it is natural for all liberals to assault the human spirit. As humans, we all have an innate yearning to want to create, achieve, and overcome. However, liberals continually barrage individuals with negative messages to discourage them from reaching their full human potential. If you are poor, a liberal will do everything in his power to persuade you that you have no chance of climbing the economic ladder and, therefore, need the assistance of liberal government programs just to survive. If you did not attend college or least complete high school, a liberal will say you are only qualified to perform menial jobs. If you have a dream to accomplish a personal goal (climb the highest mountain, open a business, invent a new product, etc.), a liberal will dissuade you with warnings of it being too dangerous, too costly, or too risky.

Chapter 5: Where do we go from here?

Now that I have exposed the young child inside every liberal, you should be able to identify one in person, on TV, and in publication. Since you now know what liberals are all about, you may be asking yourself, where do we go from here? Bear in mind that a liberal has a child inside himself that does not want to and probably cannot grow up. Therefore, use caution when discussing sensible topics with liberals. If during a conversation, a liberal begins to have a cry-baby moment, do not take it personally. It is the only reaction liberals are capable of, since they are incapable of participating in a rational argument.

What you need to be aware of is that liberals will do anything in their power to convince people to be ashamed of living the American lifestyle. You must always be suspicious when a liberal claims looming disaster, calamity, or imminent danger. Be very skeptical when you read or hear on the news about the results of some study claiming perilous outcomes if certain activities are not immediately regulated or curbed. I am sure you have heard or read a laundry list of studies claiming that if you eat particular foods or participate in specified activities, you will get some horrible disease or die prematurely. My advice is to ignore liberals and live your life the way you wish. If I could recommend that you banish your liberal friends to the corner of the room for a timeout or give them a good spanking on the behind, I would. However, such actions are contrary to the function of a civil and polite society. Thus, it is best to go along with your liberal friends and let them believe you have finally *seen the light* that they have shined upon you. Let them be convinced they have forever changed your viewpoint to the liberal *dark side*.

Also, it is paramount to keep liberals away from powerful positions, such as policymaking and enforcement within government. For this reason, it is important to vote against *all* liberals seeking public office, from the top of the ticket all the way down to city dog-catcher. Regrettably, there will always be a quantity of liberals who worm their way into various positions and levels of government. However, if we can keep them in the minority, the less their impact will be on the daily lives of all Americans.

It is imperative to never forget that all liberals are liberal, first and foremost, before they are anything else. Regardless of their nationality, religion, race, creed, or socio-economic status, to liberals, being and acting liberal is more important than being: a husband, a wife, a parent, a Christian, a Jew, an Atheist, an American, or anything else for that matter. Consequently, the liberal mantra of *no, don't, won't, banned, or not allowed* takes precedence in their baby-like minds. Keep in mind that liberals always like to tell you that you *shouldn't* or *can't* do this or that. However, liberal advice or admonishment never seems to apply to themselves. Lastly, do not forget that liberals long for the days when they were young and their parents took care of all their wants and needs. Liberals want you also to live out the same childish fantasy. The only time liberals will ever be happy is when everyone else is equally miserable. Let us hope that liberals never become happy. Within the Bible, Isaiah 11:6 states "And a little Child shall lead them." I am all for that as long as the child leading is not a liberal!

About the Author

Anthony Sebastiano was born and raised in Jamestown, New York. He served honorably in the U.S. Navy, both as an officer and enlisted man. During his nearly eight years of service, Anthony was assigned to both sea and shore tours and awarded several military decorations, including the *Navy & Marine Corps Achievement Medal*. He has earned several academic degrees including a Bachelor of Arts in Political Science (summa cum laude) from the *State University of New York, College at Fredonia* and a Master of Arts in Political Science (with a concentration in *American Politics and Government*) from the *American Military University*. As a certified pistol instructor through the National Rifle Association, Anthony fully supports and promotes the Second Amendment by teaching others how to safely and responsibly use handguns. Living in Eastern Panhandle of West Virginia with his wife, Kimberly, and a British Shorthair cat named Sadie, Anthony spends his leisure time learning to play the piano, preparing homemade cuisine, target shooting, and spending quiet time at home.

www.ingramcontent.com/pod-product-compliance
Lightning Source LLC
Chambersburg PA
CBHW021242280526
45784CB00005B/2207